WHITE QUEEN

STORIES OF FAITH AND FAME
Edited by Cecil Northcott

WHITE QUEEN

The Story of Mary Slessor

by
DONALD McFARLAN

LUTTERWORTH PRESS
GUILDFORD AND LONDON

First published 1955
Eighth impression 1965
Ninth impression 1967
Tenth impression 1970
Eleventh impression 1972
Twelfth impression 1977

ISBN 0 7188 0857 6

PRINTED PHOTOLITHO IN GREAT BRITAIN
BY EBENEZER BAYLIS AND SON, LTD.
THE TRINITY PRESS, WORCESTER, AND LONDON.

CONTENTS

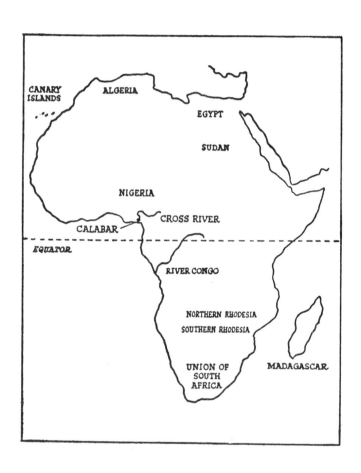

CANARY
ISLANDS

ALGERIA

EGYPT

SUDAN

NIGERIA

CROSS RIVER

CALABAR

EQUATOR

RIVER CONGO

NORTHERN RHODESIA

SOUTHERN RHODESIA

UNION OF
SOUTH
AFRICA

MADAGASCAR

1

THE WEAVER OF DREAMS

FROM her very earliest days Mary Slessor had heard about Calabar. She was born in Aberdeen on December 2, 1848, two years after the founding of the Calabar Mission in West Africa. Even as a child Mary knew the story of that thrilling adventure off by heart. She could tell how the ex-slaves of the plantations in Jamaica planned to send some of their missionaries back to their African homeland, how her own Church in Scotland adopted them, and how the pennies of poor people like her mother were helping to do God's work among the black folk.

The most exciting day in the month was the day her mother brought home the *Missionary Record* from the church and read out the latest news from their very own mission field. Mary and her brothers and sisters listened and listened while Mrs. Slessor told them about faraway Calabar.

"'Our school is increasing a little,'" she read. "'There were very few at school when we came. Now there are between thirty and forty daily, but nearly all boys. All that we can do we cannot get the girls to attend. I once had a decent class of girls sewing, and now only two. They attend for a few days till they get frocks, and then come no more. The parents do not care about the girls learning to read. They are all exceedingly anxious to get clothes. As we have more boys than girls, I had some trouble getting shirts enough, and we have in some cases to suit out a boy in a girl's frock, as there are more girls' than boys' dresses sent. How proud they are of them!—they do not know the difference.'

"That's a letter from Mrs. Anderson," said Mary's mother. "She and her husband live in Duke Town, Calabar. Listen, here's some more . . . 'Mr. Anderson has been doing all he can to get meetings with the people in this town. He goes out at nine o'clock on the Sabbath mornings and holds meetings in the gentlemen's yards and gets someone who understands English to interpret. Sometimes the interpreter will only tell as much as he thinks proper. They do not wish the slaves to know much, and there are generally a great many slaves present. Pray for us, dear young friends, that God will keep and bless us in this dark land, and make us useful to these poor heathen.' "

Mary sighed. She longed to be a missionary. But she was small and delicate, and only the strongest of the strong, it was said, could stand up to the climate of West Africa . . . the White Man's Grave, as they called it. Meanwhile she played at keeping a school, just like the one at Duke Town, and all the imaginary boys and girls in it were black.

When Mary Slessor was ten years old the family went to live in Dundee. Her father was a shoe-maker, but in Aberdeen he could not make enough money at his trade to support the growing house-hold. Dundee at this time was attracting workers from all over the country. It had been famous as a weaving centre for a long time, but by 1859, when the Slessor family arrived there, the once neat little town by the banks of the Tay had grown to be a sprawling city full of busy mills where the raw jute from India was woven into sacks and cloth. It was one of the most over-crowded towns in all Britain, and many of the tall tenements were dark and dismal slums.

There was work for everyone in Dundee, even for the children. Mary's father got a job as a labourer in one of the mills, while her mother became a weaver. At the age of eleven Mary her-self began work as a "half-timer", attending school half the day and toiling in the mill for the other half. Within a year or two she was a full-time skilled weaver, earning a good wage. Up at five every morning, she helped with the housework before going to the mill at six. With one hour off for breakfast and an hour for lunch, she laboured there until six at night.

There was little time to think about Calabar amidst the clattering looms of the weaving shed. Sometimes Mary carried a book with her to the mill and snatched a glance at it in her free moments. But Sunday was the day when she could allow her thoughts to roam. On Sunday there was the Sabbath School and later the Bible Class, as well as regular attendance at church. She was not content merely to listen. She wanted to do something for others. If she could not go out to Africa to teach black boys and girls, at least she could take a class of children in the slums of Dundee.

*   *   *

It was easier to plan than to carry out. The boys and girls of the tenements were as wild as any heathen savages. Most of them went to no school, and, outside factory hours, they roamed the streets in noisy gangs, taking orders from no one. They made fun of the attempt to teach them, and tried to wreck the meeting-place. They followed the teachers down the street, jeering at them and throwing mud. Once they caught Mary by herself and surrounded her. The leader of the young roughs had a lead weight at the end of a string which he swung round and round her head, hoping that she would scream in terror. But Mary stood her ground, looking at the bully with steady eyes. After a little he gave up, and the whole gang went to her meeting. By her sheer courage Mary Slessor won their hearts.

*   *   *

For fourteen years she toiled in the mill. Her father died, and her mother was not strong enough to go on working, so Mary became the main support of the home. Weaving filled her working hours and all her spare time was taken up with teaching in Sabbath School and evening classes. But Africa and Calabar were still in her thoughts. Even as she ran down the street to the mill early in the morning her mind was full of the Calabar scene as she had read about it in the *Missionary Record*:

"Did I ever give you a description of our home in Calabar?" it ran. "Our house is built on a hill, about 200 feet high, rising as it were right out of the river, so that we look down on the hulks and ships; and on the top it is table-land extending far away. We have about an acre of ground around the house, enclosed by a thick hedge of limes, which is always fresh and green. There is a flower garden in front, and a number of fruit trees planted in rows by Mr. Anderson who generally takes his spade every morning from six to seven, which is the hour for worship. Under these trees, which are all large now, is a beautiful walk, always cool and shaded by the trees. The fruit trees are oranges and mangoes, bread-fruit, soursop, custard apple, coconuts, cashew, palms of different kinds . . . date palms, oil palms, and so on, and a fine bamboo in the corner. Also pineapples in abundance beside the hedge, growing, but not yet in fruit.

"The road from Duke Town to Henshaw Town and other villages passes just outside our fence. Then on the other side of the road opposite our gate are the church and school-house (a church on Sabbath, a school-house during the week), the printing office, Mrs. Sutherland's house, and Miss Edgerley's. Then houses of some of the native Christians beyond them. At the back of the mud-walled house we have out-rooms for the house-children, not near enough to be disturbed with their talk, but near enough that I can see what is going on. We have generally a large household— some orphans that were brought to us when a few months old, too young to be reared by native women. Such they used to bury with their dead mothers till we took them. We do not find time to weary with so many to look after.

"We rise at five or six o'clock, according to the light we have, for we make the most of the mornings, and there is only one hour of difference between the longest and the shortest day. All except the infants are employed till seven, when the bell rings for worship; breakfast sharp at eight; children off to school at eight-thirty. I give out coppers for the marketing, for we cannot get any quantity to buy at one time, and there is a daily marketing. We attend to other household duties till one, when we dine, and all who are able for work are employed sewing chiefly, or knitting and crochet work. At three o'clock to school till five. If no sick people in the house, I go to the town to the gentlemen's yards and teach their wives and daughters to read, and also religious instruction, for they are not allowed to attend public meetings."

As the Dundee factory looms clacked and clattered they seemed to be saying "Calabar! Calabar! Calabar!" It was not the glamour of that sun-filled land that called to Mary Slessor. It was the need. What was it Mr. Anderson had written? "Unless help be sent soon in the shape of one or two vigorous, valorous young men—if accompanied by young women of kindred spirit and energy, so much the better—I fear that ground will be lost rather than gained at Duke Town." He told, too, of the death from fever of one of the finest women workers in the Mission: "She was tall and slender . . . too narrow-shouldered for this climate. I warned the Mission Board that she was not a fit subject for Africa. A hundred others—*with broad shoulders and expansive chest*—might live here as well as at home, with occasional trips to any cold region."

"And I'm wee and thin and not very strong," said Mary to herself. "I doubt Mr. Anderson wouldn't think much of me as a missionary!" But as she worked she wove her dreams. As if to prove to herself how strong she was, she took charge of two large looms in the factory, working twice as hard as before. But still she told no one of her ambition.

Then, in 1874, the news swept through Britain of the lonely death in Africa of David Livingstone, Scotland's greatest missionary. Mary Slessor remembered her hero's words to the students of Cambridge University: "I direct your attention to Africa," Livingstone had said. "I know in a few years I shall be cut off in that country which is now open. Do not let it be shut again. I go back to Africa to try to make an open path for Commerce and Christianity. Do you carry out the work I have begun. I leave it with you!"

Mary made up her mind. In May 1875 she wrote a letter to the Foreign Mission Board of her Church, offering her services as a missionary in Calabar. Her mother gladly approved, and the Board soon learned from Dundee of Mary's character and worth. A few months later she was no longer a mill-girl in Dundee. She was a student in the Training College in Edinburgh, learning to be a teacher.

At the age of twenty-eight she set sail for Calabar. It was August 5, 1876. Just over a month later the swift iron steam-ship *Ethiopia* came to anchor in the mud-coloured waters of the Calabar River, just below Duke Town. Mary Mitchell Slessor had arrived in the land of her dreams. It was to be her home for almost forty years.

2

DREAM COME TRUE

MARY SLESSOR'S first days in Africa were full of delight. She lived in the Andersons' home in Duke Town, Calabar, a hot iron building which had been sent out in sections from her native Scotland. From the veranda the whole of the African town was in view, an untidy collection of mud huts with their mat roofs huddled in the valley between two hills. Below the town was the shining river, bustling with dug-out canoes, and across the water stretched mile upon mile of unknown forest, dark and mysterious.

The people of the Calabar towns did a profitable trade in palm oil with the European traders who visited the river. The whole of the surrounding country was dotted with oil palms which grew wild. When the heavy clusters of palm nuts were red ripe they were cut down and boiled up in great iron pots. The rich oil was skimmed off the pots and put into huge barrels or "puncheons", to be ferried out by canoe to the waiting ships. The European traders lived on board their "hulks" as they were called. To Mary they looked like the Noah's arks of nursery pictures. They were sailing ships with masts bare of canvas, their decks completely roofed over for the time being with native mats as a protection against the drenching tropical rain. Month after month they lay swinging at anchor in the river, slowly taking in puncheons of palm oil. Then, when their holds were full, the mats were torn down, the sails run up, and the ships made for the open sea, homeward bound.

There was no time for day-dreaming in the mission house. Everyone got up at first light, before six o'clock, and Mrs. Anderson gave them their duties for the day. The house was full of people. Mrs. Anderson's right-hand helper was an African girl called Julia who saw to the orderly running of the household. The cook had the unusual name of Mary Stewart. Both girls had been with Mammy Anderson for many years and were devoted to her. But apart from these regular servants, there were about a dozen boys and girls of all ages who helped to run errands, carry water from the spring, and look after the pet goats, fowls, dogs and cats which swarmed everywhere in the mission yard.

Some of the African children were twins, and Mary Slessor soon learned why they were there. The Efik people of Calabar were terrified of twins. They believed that they were children of the devil, and a twin mother was driven from her home in horror as soon as her babies were born. Usually the tiny bodies of the twins were broken and crushed into pots to be cast into the bush or thrown in the river. The mothers themselves were outcasts. But in Duke Town, at least, thanks to the missionaries, there was a home for such mothers and children in the mission yard. One of Mary's first tasks was to care for the tiny black babies who were brought, often at dead of night, to the sanctuary of the mission.

Mammy Anderson, as the people called her, was a strict manager of her large and varied household. She told Mary that her first job every morning would be to get up before dawn and ring a warning bell for morning prayers. It was the custom in Calabar to ring the first bell at five o'clock, the second at six, and another at seven, when prayers were held. The big iron bell had been presented to the mission by a former "king" of Duke Town called Eyamba, and it hung in a fork of a tree beside the church. As she tugged at the rope and heard the clang-clang, clang-clang float out over the sleeping town Mary thought of the factory hooters which used to waken the weavers of Dundee. How far away it all seemed!

Sometimes she slept in, and Mammy Anderson was angry. Punctuality was her watchword for all the duties of the day. Mary found, too, that everyone must be in time for meals. When she was late, not for the first time, Mammy Anderson told her sharply that she would get no food, as a punishment. Mary went to her own room in silence. A little later there was a knock at the door. It was Mr. Anderson himself.

"Why were you late again to-day, Miss Slessor?" he asked gravely.

"I walked through the bush to Old Town," said Mary. "There was no way of telling the time. I'm sorry I was late for dinner."

She hesitated. "I climbed a tree and sat in the branches for a time," she confessed. "It was fun, watching the people coming and going along the bush path, and none of them knowing I was there. I'm afraid that's the real reason I was late."

"Climbing trees!" exclaimed Mr. Anderson. "Do you think that was a dignified thing for a lady missionary to do? What would Mammy Anderson say if she heard that?"

His eyes twinkled. "See, I have brought you some biscuits and bananas," he said. "That will keep you going until supper time. And I'll tell you a secret. I remember a girl in Jamaica, a young mission teacher like yourself. She was a great one for climbing trees, too. She was full of spirits, roaming over the hills of Jamaica like a wild deer. Well, that was almost forty years ago, when she was just twenty-two. But she's got far too much to do nowadays to waste time climbing trees. Think of the house to run, and the women's yards to visit, and the twin-mothers to attend to."

"You mean Mammy Anderson?" said Mary in amazement.

Mr. Anderson nodded. "But don't tell her I told you," he said. "You must help her all you can, like a good lassie. There's so much to do, and so few folk to do it. Some day, perhaps, you'll be all on your own, with hundreds of the Africans depending on you. I'm sure you'll remember then how much Mammy Anderson does every day."

As the days passed Mary was busy from morning to night. As Mr. Anderson had said, there was so much to do! She had to learn the Efik language, for instance, so that she could talk to the Calabar women when she visited them in their own homes. It was difficult at first to get her Scots tongue round some of the strange words. Mr. Goldie, the pioneer missionary at Creek Town, gave her a copy of the Efik dictionary which he had made up, and she followed the lessons in church in her Efik Bible. The hymns, at least, weren't so strange, for they were sung to the tunes she had learned at Sunday School and church in Scotland. But she soon found that the easiest way to learn Efik was to speak it as much as possible, even if she did make mistakes at first. Soon she was able to chatter to the twins and the servant girls in the house and

to try out her new language in the market-place.
The people were delighted. "She talks like a
Calabar woman," they said.

Mary learned how treacherous the climate was.
She went from one native compound to another
under the hot sun and came back to the mission
utterly exhausted. Occasional bouts of fever left
her weak for days on end. It was then that she
realised how kind and gentle Mammy Anderson
was.

*　　*　　*

Sometimes Mary was impatient with everyone
and everything. The Duke Town compounds
were filthy, and the children covered with sores.
More than half the babies born in the place died
before they reached the age of one, just because
of dirt and the ignorance and carelessness of the
mothers. The women received her in their mud
huts willingly enough, and listened patiently while
she talked to them. But they did not change their
ways. When Mary Slessor urged them to keep
their homes tidy, to give up their superstitions,
they shrugged their shoulders and said: "It is our
custom." She longed to shake them, to turn the
whole town upside down and drive out the evil
and filth.

She had to learn to control her own restless,

eager spirit. "It is difficult to wait," she wrote home. "But there's one text I keep remembering: 'Learn of Me.' Christ was never in a hurry. There was no rushing forward or anticipating, no fretting over what might be. Every day's duties were done as every day brought them, and the rest was left with God."

Her main task lay in the day-school, near the mission house in Duke Town. There were about fifty children, mainly boys. Their fathers hoped that if they "learned book" they would make all the better traders with the ships' captains in the river. Mary taught them to read and write, using for reading books the Efik translation of the Bible and the *Pilgrim's Progress* and *Shorter Catechism*. On Sundays her young scholars came with her to church and Sunday School. There was a regular attendance of more than eight hundred worshippers at the Sunday services.

Many of the Duke Town people made their farms a few miles inland from the river and came back to the town only when the wet season made outdoor work impossible. Throughout most of the year they toiled on the land, clearing the bush with their primitive knives and hoes and tending their crops of yams, cassava, peppers and maize. Whenever she could, Mary Slessor trekked through the forest to visit them. Usually she carried with her a few simple medicines and bandages, for there was always someone sick or wounded. There was no doctor or nurse to attend to them when they were ill, and if they consulted the witch-doctor he plastered their sores with evil-smelling messes of mud and leaves.

Mary came to realise how greatly fear over-shadowed the lives of the Efik people. Any accident or sickness was attributed to the work of an evil spirit or to an ill-disposed neighbour. The witch-doctor was consulted, and he proceeded to "smell out" the enemy. He would crouch on the ground with his bag of charms, muttering to himself as he threw bits of bones this way and that, while everyone watched in fearful silence. Suddenly he would pounce, usually on a woman or girl, and accuse her of causing the sickness. The terrified creature was then ordered to "chop nut", that is, to undergo the poison bean ordeal. The Calabar, or *esere* bean was ground into powder, mixed with water, and the victim had to swallow the poisonous draught. If she vomited the mixture she was held to be innocent. If not, she died in fearful agony, and everyone was convinced that she must have been guilty. Not once, but many times, Mary Slessor saw the dreadful rite, but protest as she might, the people clung obstinately to their custom.

*   *   *

In June 1879 she returned to Scotland on her first furlough, tired out and more than a little home-sick. But as she recovered strength her thoughts turned continually to Calabar. Already she wanted to be on her own, to get away from the regular routine of life in Duke Town and to work in the unknown bush inland from the riverside towns. Mr. Anderson did not approve of the idea. Pioneering was not for a woman. The dangers and difficulties were too great. But when Mary returned to West Africa in 1880 she was happy to find that she was to be allowed to take charge of Old Town, about two miles above Duke Town, and that she would live on her own.

Her new home was utterly different from the tidy, well-furnished mission house on Duke Town hill. It was a dilapidated, mat-roofed mud hut, with only the simplest of furniture. But Mary was free to order her own life, and she was so busy all day long that she became quite indifferent both to comfort and to the company of her own folk. Day in day out she taught in the mud-walled schools which had been put up in Old Town and in other nearby villages. Young and old alike attended as scholars. In one of the villages the head man sat on a low bench alongside the small children and chanted his A.B.C. along with them.

Sunday was her busiest day. It began very early in the morning with a trek through the forest to an outlying village to hold a service. Two boys went with her, carrying a large bell slung between them on a pole, to call the people to worship. Then on to another village for another service. After worship in each place she would visit one home after another and talk with the women. Then back to Old Town for her Sunday School in the afternoon.

At night, in the welcome coolness that followed the heat of the day, she held a meeting in the open air, in the chief's compound. A table covered with a white cloth was her pulpit, and on it was an oil lamp and a Bible. She would read a passage to the silent villagers and explain it, pray with them and for them, and then lead her scholars in singing some Efik hymns. At last, under a silver moon and a tropical sky full of stars, the people would accompany her to her house, tired but happy.

"Tie-suño!" they would call in the Efik tongue. ("Rest softly!") And "Saña-suño!" ("Go softly!") she would reply as they made for their own mud huts nearby.

Mary Slessor began to make exploring trips by canoe up the Cross River. Wherever she went she carried medicines and bandages with her. Even where the people might be afraid of the fair-haired, white-skinned stranger, they came to respond to her gentle touch as she bound up wounds and soothed pain. On one such trip a violent tornado broke over the river on the homeward journey and when the canoe crept into the beach near Old Town Mary was so ill with fever that she had to be carried up the hill to her house. Not long after, in the spring of 1883, she was sent home under doctor's orders. She took with her a girl-twin whom she had rescued and who was to become her faithful servant and friend to the end of her days. The black, curly-headed baby girl was baptised in Mary's old Sunday School in Dundee, and called Janie, after her own youngest sister.

Twelve years after she had first set foot in Duke Town, the local mission committee gave in to Mary's repeated pleading and agreed to send her inland to a new mission station. During those years in Calabar she had gleaned a good deal of information about the tribes of the interior. She knew, for example, that the Efiks would not allow the up-river people to trade with the oil-ships at Duke Town. They wanted to keep all the profit to themselves. She knew, too, that there had been war time and time again between the men of Duke Town and the chiefs of Okoyong, Umon, and other places inland.

Okoyong especially interested her. One of the

missionaries, T. W. Campbell, had explored on foot far inland and had come back from one trip with a troop of Okoyong boys who had been sent to school at Creek Town. He told Mary about his travels and about the stalwart, warlike people whom he had met. "They will trust no man from Efik country," he warned her. "Inside or outside, speaking, eating, or sleeping, they have their guns always ready for use. If anyone is ever to win their confidence, it must be a missionary."

Mary was more and more determined that Okoyong was to be her work. At last, in 1888, the mission committee yielded to her. She was forty years old, slightly-built, often weak with fever, not physically the stuff of which pioneers are made. But she had the spirit to dare anything. Her mother and sisters had died a short time before, and often she felt very much alone. "Heaven is now nearer to me than Britain," she wrote, "and no one will be anxious about me if I go up-country."

Her Calabar friends shook their heads doubtfully.

"It's a gun-boat they need, not a missionary," said the European traders. "Remember, there is no law there, and there will be no one to rescue you if you get into trouble."

"Not a woman's job at all," was the opinion of her fellow-missionaries.

"Too lonely, and too dangerous. What will happen when you fall sick?"

The chiefs of Calabar added their voices. "Do you think anyone will listen to you there?" they said. "We'll never see you again. You'll be murdered!"

"I'm going!" said Mary Slessor. And on August 4, 1888, she set out.

3

WITH THE WARRIORS OF OKOYONG

THE journey to Okoyong was made through driving rain. All Mary Slessor's worldly possessions were in the long dug-out canoe as well as five African children and herself. The stalwart paddlers bent to their task, but progress against the strong current of the river was slow, painfully slow. It was almost dark when they reached the beach, with four miles still to go on foot through the rain-drenched forest. The children were in tears as they stumbled and floundered along the muddy track among the trees. Mary's courage and faith alone kept her going.

Even when they arrived at Ekenge, one of the Okoyong towns, there was no welcome. The people were away "celebrating" the funeral of a local chief's mother. That meant that they would be drunk for days on end. Mary put the children to sleep in a native hut, and wearily made her way back to the river to rouse the paddlers to carry her boxes of food and other supplies to her new home. It was after midnight before she was able to fling herself down to sleep, aching in every limb and sad at heart.

Her first home at Ekenge was a filthy room in a corner of the women's yard owned by Edem the chief. The place was alive with rats and cockroaches, and so cramped was the space that her boxes and chairs had to be put out of doors every night to leave room for Mary and her family to sleep. The people never left her alone for a moment. They crowded round her door, peering in at the children and her, commenting loudly on her appearance, her dress, her possessions. One of the women especially attracted Mary Slessor's attention. She was Ma Eme, a huge fat woman, sister of the chief, who had considerable power over the others. She saw to it that Mary got food, and helped her to get to know the strange folk among whom she had come to live.

"Our first visits to the Okoyong towns were not particularly cheering," Mary Slessor wrote to a friend. "Everybody seemed afraid to meet us, and when we did get them gathered together they were armed to the teeth." The Okoyong people trusted no man, not even one another, and they never went about unarmed. The only time they forgot their quarrels was when a "big man" died and they gathered together to drink and feast. All that Mary Slessor had ever read or heard or seen of heathenism was here: witchcraft, the poison ordeal, twin-murder and head-hunting.

Mary started a school at Ekenge and at Ifako,

two miles away. At first her scholars were of all ages, drawn by curiosity to see what the white "Ma" was up to. Then the older folk lost interest, and gave up, leaving her with the children. She taught them to draw their first letters in the sand, or on rough pieces of board. They learned verses of Scripture off by heart, and went home at night to recite them in the village compounds. Every school-day ended with worship. Mary taught them the Efik hymns to many a familiar Scottish psalm tune. One of her favourites was a hymn she had made up herself:

"Esiere Mufan mi, O Esiere nde,
Ikot Jesus ifekheke ekim ye okoneyo.
Ima ye emem Esie ofuk nyin nte mba.
Usiere enyene nyin, edide uwem edide mkpa."

In English the words mean:

"Good night, my friends, O again good night,
The Jesus folk fear not darkness and night.
His love and His peace shield us like a wing,
The Light is ours, come life or death."

They sang it to the lilting Scottish tune: *Rothesay Bay.*

Slowly, very slowly, the people of Okoyong came to respect the white stranger in their midst.

She was often sent for when they were sick, and she never failed to go, by day or night. If she could save the life of a sick man or woman she might preserve a whole village from the poison ordeal. Even Edem, the chief of Ekenge, began to turn to her for advice.

*　　*　　*

On one occasion Mary heard that there was going to be fighting between two villages of Okoyong. She went at once to Edem's house and talked with him, deliberately keeping him at home. Towards dark he grew more and more uneasy, and suggested that it was time for her to go back to her own household.

"Oh, I'm quite comfortable here," said Mary brightly.

After a bit he tried again.

"Ma, you'll get sick of fever in the night air if you wait here."

"Would you care if I died?" replied Mary quietly. "Edem, my friend, I know what your people are planning to-night. I know they expect you to lead them. But remember, you promised me that you would not fight. That is why I must stay here, to see that you keep your word."

Edem got up in silence and went to his own quarters. Mary Slessor called urgently for Ma

Eme. "I shall sleep here," she said. "But if chief Edem makes any move, wake me at once."

In the middle of the night she felt a hand on her shoulder. In the glimmer of the moonlight she could make out the huge bulk of Ma Eme bending over her. The African woman said nothing, but pointed to the open doorway. Quickly Mary swung out of bed and went out. All was still in the compound, but on the fringe of the forest she caught up with chief Edem, sword in hand. She knew that the bush was full of armed men waiting for him to lead them.

"Where are you going, chief?" she asked.

"I'm just going for a walk," he replied.

"Good, I'll go with you," said Mary Slessor calmly.

Without further words they walked through the forest together, following one twisting track after another. At last they turned back to the compound, and Mary knew that there would be no fighting that night. For a whole week she watched Edem, day and night, never letting him far out of her sight. At last he came and laid his sword at her feet.

"Monyime, Ma" ("I am willing, Ma"), he said, and she knew that she had won. The warrior had yielded to the missionary.

*   *   *

After a time the people helped her to build a house for herself and her African family. It was of woven bamboo, plastered with mud, with the usual mat roof. In one of the two rooms she made a sideboard of mud, smoothed and polished with a stone, and a mud sofa. The other room held her boxes, books and bed. Next, a roomy native building was put up at Ifako for her daily work. It was "Ufok Nwed" (The House of the Book) all week, but on Sunday it was "Ufok Abasi" (The House of the Lord).

About a year after Mary Slessor first arrived in Okoyong, the mission committee sent Mr. Ovens, a missionary carpenter, to help her to build a permanent house. Thus they acknowledged the value of her work. Ekenge was to be a full-fledged mission station. Mr. Ovens arrived on a Monday, to find Mary holding a church service.

"Why are you travelling on Sunday?" was her greeting.

He gazed at her in amazement. "To-day is Monday," he said. "Yesterday was Sunday. I'm quite sure of it, for I was twice at the kirk in Duke Town." Mary looked abashed. "I've lost track of the days," she confessed. "Well, the people here think it's Sunday, so you'll just have to have two Sundays this week!"

Next morning Mr. Ovens got to work on the

new building, a proper mission house with doors and windows, a veranda, kitchen and dispensary. He was quite new to the country, and this was his first job. He soon learned that anything might happen in Okoyong and in the company of Mary Slessor. Again and again someone brought word that twins had been born, or that there was a drunken riot going on, or that someone had been accused of witchcraft and was facing the poison ordeal. Many a time the Scots carpenter found that he had to lay down his tools and take charge of a household of black children while Mary rushed off to the rescue.

One morning he was hammering away when he saw Mary Slessor disappear into the forest.

"What's going on this time?" he said to himself. "I wish I knew the language of this country. You never know what's going to happen next!"

He called his Calabar assistant and told him to run after Ma Slessor.

In a short time the boy came back hot-foot with a message that there had been an accident.

"Ma says, come quickly, and bring medicines," he gasped.

Mr. Ovens found Mary kneeling beside the body of a young African while a crowd of villagers watched and wailed round about.

"It's Etim, the son of chief Edem," she explained rapidly in English. "He has been struck by a falling tree. I'm afraid it's serious. He's unconscious now, and I'm just afraid his neck is broken. If he dies . . ." She did not finish the sentence, but the carpenter read her thoughts. The death of so important a man would start a reign of terror all over the district.

Mr. Ovens and his boy made a rough stretcher and carried the unconscious youth back to Ekenge, to his mother's house. For two weeks Mary visited him continually, praying for his recovery. But one Sunday morning she found the dying man being held up by his relatives while they tried frantically to call his fleeting spirit back to the body. They blew smoke in his nostrils, rubbed searing pepper in his eyes, shouted desperately in his ears. But the dead feel not and hear not. As Etim fell back to the ground, lifeless, a great wail went up from the watchers. Chief Edem was beside himself with fear and rage. "He has been killed by witch-craft!" he shouted. "Bring the witch-doctor and let him declare who has done this!"

Panic spread through the village at his words, and men, women and children fled to the forest. No one knew who might be the first to be accused. But the witch-doctor declared that another village was to blame for Etim's death and chief Edem called out his armed men. They moved swiftly in on the offending place, seized everyone they could find, dragged them back in chains to Edem's yard, and tied them up.

It was then that Mr. Ovens saw the stuff Mary Slessor was made of. The situation was very grave, but she did not despair. She raked among the tin trunks in the mission house, bringing out a lot of old-fashioned clothes and ornaments which had come out in mission boxes from Scotland. She went to Edem the chief and told him that she grieved over the death of his son.

"I myself shall arrange his funeral," she announced. "He will have every honour befitting his rank."

She was true to her word. The body was dressed in vivid silks, with a new suit over all. Round the head went a silk turban with a black and scarlet hat on top, crowned with feathers. Strings of big brass buttons were hung round his neck. Then the body was set upright in an armchair in the women's yard under a gaudy umbrella. As a final touch, Mary Slessor placed a mirror before Etim to reflect his splendour. The people were astounded and delighted. Never before had there been such a splendid sight in Okoyong. They danced in a wild frenzy round the corpse, firing guns and singing the merits of the departed youth.

The days and nights passed in an orgy of drinking and feasting. But Mary Slessor knew well that the danger was not yet over. The wretched prisoners were still in chains, drooping from posts along the veranda of the chief's house. *Esere* beans were being pounded and prepared for the poison ordeal on a large scale. Wearily but patiently Miss Slessor and Mr. Ovens took turn about on watch, he by day and she by night.

The crowd grew wilder. They faced Mary Slessor with hostile cries when she insisted that there must be no poisoning. "Bring our master back to life," they cried, "and you can have the prisoners."

In the middle of the night the crisis came. A woman prisoner was unchained and thrust before the dead Etim to drink the poison. Her guards were reeling with drink, and Mary saw her chance. She clutched the terrified woman by the arm and called on her to run. Together they sped through the dark compounds to the safety of the mission yard. Leaving Mr. Ovens to guard the woman, Mary Slessor returned to the drunken crowd. For hours she argued and begged for the lives of the other captives. At long last Edem gave in. Etim was buried with the sacrifice of a cow instead of with a retinue of slaves for the spirit world. It was the first time in the history of Okoyong that there had been no human sacrifice on the death of a man of rank.

*   *   *

Mary Slessor often recalled what she had written in the letter from Duke Town, years before: "Christ was never in a hurry . . . every day's duties were done as every day brought them, and the rest was left with God." In her Master's spirit of trust and patience she lived and worked. There was no spectacular Christian victory over a pagan people to report, no crowded churches or model schools. There was not as yet one single Church member from the whole of Okoyong. But her influence over the tribe was enormous. Chiefs sought her advice. She was law-giver, teacher, healer and friend of everyone. In Ma Slessor they saw the love of God in action.

She used to take her many African visitors into her own house and show them her simple possessions. The naked women admired and fingered the missionary's clothes, her curtains and bed-covers. They chattered with delight at the sight of pots and pans and dishes. The men marvelled at the ticking clock that told the time of day. A looking-glass was a thing of wonder. They tasted the condensed milk which Mary kept for the babies, and the strange white sugar, and pronounced them "Sweet too much!" with loud grunts of approval.

Noting their interest, Mary wrote letters to some of her trading friends in Calabar asking them to bring up market-goods by canoe, promising that her people would be eager to buy them. But the Efiks, fearing for their lives, would not venture up-river. Mary wrote again, this time to the Christian king Eyo VII of Creek Town, begging him to invite some of the Okoyong chiefs to visit him. He did so, and very suspiciously the chiefs went down-river, their white "Ma" with them. The king received them with great kindness, showed them all his goods, and promised to open up trade. From that time Okoyong developed a profitable market for their palm oil and crops. In exchange, all kinds of new and wonderful trade goods found their way to Ekenge and Ifako and the other villages of the inland tribe. There was less time for drinking and fighting.

When she first set out for Okoyong Mary Slessor had written: "I am going to a new tribe up-country, a fierce, cruel people, and everyone tells me that they will kill me. But I don't fear any hurt—only to combat their savage customs will require courage and firmness on my part." In a few years she was their acknowledged queen, and the warlike people had laid their weapons at her feet. Her victory came from courage, love and prayer.

4

IN THE NAME OF THE QUEEN

ONCE in a while Mary Slessor went down-river to Calabar to enjoy the company of her own folk. Her whole household of children went with her, for there was never a time when she did not have unwanted twins or orphans to nurse and care for. Her friends in Creek Town or Duke Town gave her a warm welcome, and she was able to rest and dream her dreams for the days to come. Her thoughts were continually for the future, when the country would be opened up, slavery abolished, and the evils of the bush driven out. Like her hero David Livingstone, Mary Slessor was a great believer in the civilising influence of trade.

She was delighted with the changes that had taken place in Duke Town since she first landed there some fifteen years before. In those days the missionaries had been the only white folk allowed to settle there. The European traders kept to their ships in the river. The only representative of British law and order was the Consul, who was stationed on the Spanish island of

Fernando Po, off the Coast of Guinea. Occasionally he visited the Calabar River in a gun-boat to see that trade was being carried on fairly and peacefully. Though the missionaries urged the chiefs without ceasing to give up murder, slavery and wholesale poisonings, their words often went unheeded. There was no law except "It is our custom" and the Calabar chiefs had the power of life or death over their people.

But by 1891 the British Government was in control in Calabar. From the veranda of the mission house at Duke Town Mary Slessor could see the imposing government station on top of the neighbouring hill. It was the headquarters of Sir Claude Macdonald, Commissioner and Consul-General of the Niger Coast Protectorate. Calabar was now the capital of British territory.

*   *   *

One sunlit morning Mary Slessor had a visit from the Commissioner himself. He found her swaying to and fro in a rocking-chair on the veranda, a little frail lady with bright eyes. In her arms was a black baby. Other children played round about her chair while Janie kept them in order.

The missionary and the Queen's Commissioner talked together of plans for the future of the country.

"You must have seen many changes in Duke Town, Miss Slessor," said Sir Claude Macdonald.

"Aye, sir, that I have! It's a bonny sight to see proper roads in the place nowadays, and trees planted along the water-front, and folk decently dressed going quietly about their work."

"It's a slow business," confessed Sir Claude. "But the Efiks are beginning to see that the improvements are all to their advantage. Think of the old days in Calabar, only a few years ago . . . cannibalism, twin-murder, wives and slaves killed whenever a chief died, the poison ordeal. You missionaries have done great things here. Now you need me and my men to back you up.

"We've made a beginning here," he went on. "There are two sanitary inspectors in charge of Duke Town, and the streets are cleaned every day. That's a change from the old days, when you remember the filth that used to lie about, breeding disease. We've cleared the bush and drained the place, too. That should help to get rid of malaria. Why, I've a score of officers living on Government Hill, not to mention the African troops in the barracks, and we haven't had a death or serious illness in the last three years. Think of that! If we clean up the native town in the same way, what a difference it will make! Then there's a post office, and a Customs

House, and the Botanic Gardens. I've arranged to give away free gifts of coffee and cocoa plants to anyone who will promise to cultivate them. Perhaps some day we'll be exporting hundreds of tons of coffee and cocoa from Calabar, as well as palm oil.

"I want to do the same for Okoyong and the other places inland," the Commissioner continued. "I've heard a great deal about your work, Miss Slessor. If only I can continue what you have begun, we can open up the Calabar and Cross Rivers to free trade and see that there is law and order and justice for everyone, not only in Duke Town, but in the interior, too."

"How are you going to do it?" asked Mary Slessor practically. "The Okoyongs are just as suspicious of the white man as of the Efiks. I've tried to make a beginning, but I'm just a woman with one pair of hands and one pair of feet. I can't be everywhere at once. Look at my school work . . . it's just a scramble. My mission boys and girls do most of the teaching. And the palavers with the chiefs . . . they go on for hours and hours, and so little comes of it all."

Sir Claude Macdonald pointed down the hill to the river. "You see that boat?" he said. "Yes, the stern-wheeler, tied up at the new wharf. That's the *Beecroft*. She's my key to unlock the rivers. Your friends in the mission have

44

explored more than two weeks' journey up the Cross River. You already have four or five out-stations as far north as Unwana. But at any time the tribes can close the way with their quarrelling and fighting. At all costs we must keep the river open, so that the canoes can pass peacefully up and down. That's where the *Beecroft* comes in. The very sight of her means law and order. What I want to see is a peaceful waterway, so that the Efiks can carry store goods to every beach along the riverside and the inland folk can send down their palm oil and yams to Calabar."

"You're going to be busy!" said Mary drily. "But it will come, yes, it will come. Daddy Anderson used to say we should give thanks for the past and trust for the future."

"I must have your help in Okoyong," said the Commissioner. "The British Government has authorised me to appoint Vice-Consuls for the native courts which we are setting up. I know that there will be trouble if I send a strange white officer among your people. He won't know their ways, and they won't trust him. But they trust you. That is why I am asking you to be Vice-Consul in Okoyong. You will represent Her Majesty the Queen there. You will be in charge of all the affairs of the tribe and preside as magistrate in the court."

* * *

So it was arranged. Mary Slessor, the former weaver girl, became the first woman magistrate in the British Empire. She was no soft, sentimental law-giver. She could "think black", and she knew the ways and the language of the people as well as they did themselves. It was a great change for the people of Okoyong. No longer had the chiefs the power of life and death. Their whims had to yield to the law. Mary Slessor had authority to call on a strong police force from Calabar if need be. But she preferred to rely on the confidence and trust the folk placed in her as their friend. In the native court she sat knitting through the long day while she heard the court cases. She listened patiently, occasionally throwing in a searching question. Then she would sum up, and her judgment was swift and direct. She was completely master of the local language. She could make the people laugh, quoting some of their native proverbs against them. But she could cut with it, too, and make them hang their heads in shame. Sometimes she took the law quite literally into her own hands, rising indignantly to give a chief a stinging blow on the cheek for daring to lie to her. They called her their white mother. In return she expected truth and obedience from her children.

Everyone said that Mary Slessor was an unusual and sometimes very extraordinary missionary. She was shy, even timid, often fearful of the wild animals of the forest paths. Yet she would face an armed band of warriors inflamed by drink, pull the weapons from their hands, and tell them: "Go home and behave yourselves, like good laddies." Her way of life broke every rule of health for white people in the tropics. She would not use a mosquito net, nor filter the water she drank. Native food sufficed for her needs. Her hair was cropped short, like a boy's, because it needed little attention that way. She wore neither shoes nor a hat, and tramped the forest on her bare feet, oblivious to cuts and scratches and the danger of snakes.

For all that, she was a woman of great dignity. The world knows her as "Mary Slessor", but not even her most intimate friends called her by her Christian name. To her fellow-countrymen she was always "Miss Slessor"; to the Africans, "Ma Miss Slessor", or simply, "Ma", a native title of the greatest respect.

On one occasion Mr. and Mrs. Weir, missionary friends from Creek Town, came up to spend a week-end at Ekenge. They marvelled at her primitive way of life, but said nothing. Mrs. Weir went with her to an outlying village where a head man had just died. The two missionaries watched the burial of the man in a grave beneath the mud floor of his own house, according to native custom. His possessions were put in the grave with him so that he might have them handy in the world of the spirits. Mrs. Weir shook her head at such superstition after years of Christian teaching in their midst. Mary Slessor read her friend's thoughts.

"You are thinking they haven't changed much," she said. "But when I first came to Okoyong there wouldn't have been a man or woman or child in the place whose life would have been safe at a time like this. They would all have 'run for bush', as they say, at the first mention of death, and any who were caught would have been slaughtered and thrown into the grave with him."

An epidemic of small-pox swept through the villages of Okoyong, carrying off hundreds of people. Mary Slessor turned her house at Ekenge into a hospital and spent hours every day vaccinating everyone who came to her. Many already had the disease and sought her aid only in extremity. There was no one to nurse the sick or bury the dead. Chief Edem, her old enemy, caught small-pox and Mary fought for his life. But he got steadily worse, and died alone, with only the missionary by his side. All his people whom the disease had not yet claimed had fled. With her own hands Mary Slessor shaped a rough coffin, dug a grave in the deserted compound, and buried him. No one ever lived there again. The bush rapidly grew over the empty huts and vacant yards, the scene of her first home in Okoyong.

*　　*　　*

After eight years in Okoyong Mary Slessor found that her hopes were being realised. The Cross River was now a highway of peaceful trade. A market-place had been opened up at a place called Akpap, nearer the river, and the greater part of the population had moved there. She determined to follow them. Once again she was a pioneer, with a simple mud hut for her African family and herself.

In a letter home she described the daily scene in the mission compound: "Four children at my feet, listening," she wrote, "five boys outside getting a reading-lesson from Janie; a man lying on the ground who has run away from his master and is taking refuge until I get him forgiven; an old chief with a girl who has a bad ulcer; a woman begging for my intervention with her husband; a nice girl with heavy brass leglets from her knee to the ankles, with pieces of cloth wrapped round to prevent the skin being cut, whom I am teaching; and three for vaccination."

But the continual strain was telling on her health, and she was rarely free from pain. Lying

49

in bed, or on her mud couch, from which she could keep an eye on her varied household, she set down on paper an account of her years in Okoyong:

"All the children within reach are sent to the school . . . raiding, plundering, the stealing of slaves, have almost entirely ceased. Any person from any place can come now for trade or pleasure, and stay wherever they choose, their persons and property being as safe as in Calabar. For fully a year we have heard of nothing like violence from even the most backward of our people. They have thanked me for restraining them in the past, and begged me to be their consul, as they neither wished black man nor white man to be their king. One chief, who, with fierce gesticulations, some years ago protested that we must draw the line at twins, and that they should never be brought to light in his life-time, brought one of his children who was very ill, two months ago, and laid it on my knee alongside the twin already there, saying with a sob in his voice: 'There! they are all yours, living or dying, they are all yours. Do what you like with mine.' "

A great deal more she wrote as she thought on the needs of her people. So much to do, so little done! But she herself was worn out and gravely ill. In March 1898 she went home to Scotland. It was her first furlough for six long years. So weak was she that she had to be carried on board the ship at Calabar. And to Scotland she took with her some of her household from the African bush, Janie, her constant companion, and three curly-headed children all under five years of age.

5

THE LAND OF THE LONG JUJU

MARY SLESSOR was fifty years old when she returned to Akpap. The climate and the job had taken their toll of her frail body, but her spirit was as vital as ever. She had opened up Okoyong and made it safe to live in. Now her whole thought was to move on. She was essentially a pioneer, a beginner of great enterprises. It was a mark of greatness in her character that she recognised her own limitations and realised that others were needed to build up a strong Christian community. As for herself: "I would like to go further inland and make a home among a tribe of cannibals," she declared.

She pestered both government officials and missionaries for information about the tribes further up the Cross River, especially those that inhabited the land that lay inland from the west bank. But no one could tell her much. There was still a great deal of inter-tribal war and slave-dealing going on. One of the greatest slave-centres in the whole of West Africa was the Long Juju in Arochuku. Mary had heard whispers about its dreadful power from fleeing slaves who sought her protection. But it was not until the Aro Expedition of 1901 that she and her colleagues fully realised how lawless was that part of the country.

For over a hundred miles on the right bank of the Cross River the Aro people ruled supreme. Their wealth and power were due to slave-trading, and its centre was the mysterious grove of Chuku, their god. It was a terrifying place that no ordinary mortal dared approach. In a dark valley, overhung by tall trees, was the Long Juju, a rock cavern in the midst of the stream that wandered sluggishly through the ravine. The sun never penetrated to those secret depths. The priests of the cult alone knew what deeds of darkness were done there.

The terror of the Long Juju reached out far beyond the land of the Aros. There were Aro agents scattered in villages throughout the country, men who had settled down among strangers, outwardly as traders, but all in the service of Chuku. If the crops failed, or sickness swept through a village, it was to the man of Aro that the chiefs turned. His words were always the same: "Go and consult the Long Juju. Take a human sacrifice with you. Chuku will listen to your prayer and tell you what to do to protect your village from harm."

Then a helpless victim was selected, usually a strong young man or girl, for Chuku demanded the best and rejected weaklings. Emissaries led the living sacrifice by forest paths until they came to one of the towns of Arochuku. There all the strangers were blindfolded and had their hands tied behind their backs. They were led by secret ways to the grove itself. With every step their terror grew.

At the edge of the stream their eyes were uncovered. There was a small island in the midst of the waters and on it the altar of Chuku, littered with the remains of animal sacrifices and human skulls. Beyond the island was a rock cave, the entrance to which was screened from curious eyes and decorated with grinning skulls. The priests of Chuku lurked in the cave and spoke the will of their god.

Usually the strangers made an offering of a white cockerel or a sheep or goat before they consulted the oracle of the grove. Then from the hidden cavern came a booming, uncanny voice giving them the counsel they sought. The human victim was led into the shrine and disappeared for ever from his companions' sight. The latter waited and watched the waters of the stream. A few moments later it ran with blood and they knew that their offering had been accepted. Then the servants of the grove blindfolded them again and led them back to a known path beyond the bounds of Arochuku, to carry the message of Chuku back to their own people.

Such was the terrifying practice that the Aros had built up over many years. But unknown to the outsider, the human victim had not been killed in the cave. He or she was imprisoned there while the priests threw red cam-wood dye or the blood of a goat into the stream to deceive the watchers. Later the captives were herded together and marched in chains to the slave-market at Itu, where the Enyong and Cross Rivers met. Thus the Aros grew rich, not only from the sale of their many captives, but also from the huge fees they exacted from awe-struck chiefs when the oracle was asked to give judgment in village disputes.

At times, to increase the terror of the Long Juju, a message was sent throughout the land: "Chuku wants sacrifices." Then every town under Aro influence had to send youths and girls to be slaughtered. There was an orgy of cannibal feast-ing and Chuku was satisfied, for the time being.

On August 14, 1901, a runner sped barefoot through the forest of Okoyong with an important message from the High Commissioner of the Pro-tectorate of Southern Nigeria. It commanded Mary Slessor to come down to Calabar. Similar

messages had gone out to all the up-river missionaries. Mary Slessor packed up very unwillingly,
but an order was an order. She found Duke
Town and Creek Town tense with excitement.
A military expedition was being organised to
destroy the Long Juju and all the horrible cult of
Chuku. On Government Hill a field force of
150 white officers and several thousand native
troops was being drilled. The mission launch
Jubilee had been commandeered as a floating am-
bulance, while a missionary doctor and two nurses
had been attached to the expedition to care for the
wounded.

The Aro Expedition set out from Duke Town
in October, accompanied by a large band of hired
carriers and watched by the missionaries and
people of Calabar. The field force split up into
several detachments, moving inland towards Arochuku by different routes. The Aro people,
because of their excellent intelligence service,
heard of their coming long before they saw them,
and started raiding and plundering outlying
villages. At first they showed no fear of the
military forces that marched against them. The
priests of the grove had spoken wise words to
give them courage. "These white men are al-
binos," they said. "They cannot see well under
the sun. Attack them in daylight and all will
be well." They promised the chiefs of Aro

many white slaves and a great feast of human flesh.

But as the troops moved forward in trained order and the machine-guns stuttered, panic spread throughout the land of Aro. On Christmas Eve, 1901, the army camped in the forest beside the Long Juju. Explosive charges were set, the ravine was blown up, and the whole place utterly destroyed. Some of the chiefs and priests of Arochuku were captured and taken down to Calabar as hostages. The dread power of the Long Juju was broken.

*   *   *

Thus a vast new area was opened up and Mary Slessor set her heart on pioneer work among the people of Aro. She talked over her plans with a young missionary who had only recently arrived in the country, the Rev. A. W. Wilkie. He had been making a long overland journey on foot through country unknown to the white man to look for possible new centres for missionary work. Turning south, he arrived at Akpap on Christmas morning, in the year 1902.

Mary Slessor received him with open arms. A visitor, one of her own folk, on Christmas Day! She called instructions right and left: "Janie, put the kettle on! Annie, bring some water for a bath! Mary, set the table for chop!"

57

After a splash in a tin bath and a welcome breakfast, Mr. Wilkie sat on the floor and smoked his pipe while Mary Slessor went on with her morning's work, throwing eager questions at him all the while about his trek. There were four black babies, each in a separate pot filled with warm water on top of the stove. Mary was so interested in the conversation that she washed some of them twice over. At last they were lifted out, dried, kissed, and tucked up in cots made of milk boxes.

Mr. Wilkie never forgot that Christmas Day. When night fell Mary Slessor gathered all the children about her and told them the story of the first Christmas at Bethlehem. Then they sang a hymn together:

> "*Se eyen k'ufok enañ,*
> *Ye mekpemeron y'esañ.*
>
> > *K'edi Oboñ, O utibe!*
> > *Kpa Oboñ, edidem heaven . . .*"

> "*Who is He in yonder stall,*
> *At whose feet the shepherds fall?*
>
> > *'Tis the Lord, O wondrous story,*
> > *'Tis the Lord, the king of glory . . .*"

There was a little gift for each of the children,

and then they were all put safely to bed. After that the two missionaries talked far into the night.

That conversation made up Mary's mind. A few weeks later she crossed by canoe to Itu, the old slave-market at the mouth of the Enyong Creek. She took with her two young men, Esien and Effiom, and one of her mission girls, Mana, and settled them there to start a school, promising that she would visit Itu often. On her next trip there she climbed to the top of the hill overlooking the Cross River and chose a site for a permanent school and church. The Itu people welcomed her. Now that the menace of Aro was removed they were glad to think that a white missionary would visit their town and perhaps even come to live among them.

But Mary Slessor was looking beyond Itu to the hidden towns of Arochuku. In June 1903 she joined a Government launch on its way to visit the forces still stationed at Arochuku. On board was Colonel Montanaro, the officer in command of the troops, who pressed her to come and see the people of Aro for herself. It seemed to Mary Slessor an answer to prayer.

With the Colonel as guide she visited the devastated scene of the Long Juju and met the chiefs of the Aro towns. Many of them knew of her work in Okoyong. "Come and make your home with us," they begged. "We will build you

a house, a school, a church . . . anything you want."
As a beginning, she opened a small school in a
shed at Amasu, an Aro town near the Creek. It
was the spot where the troops had landed for their
attack on the Long Juju. Now it was an outpost of
the Christian Church.

Mary Slessor was quite sure that the chiefs'
welcome was a call from God to her to new
pioneer work once again. But the Church in
Scotland was alarmed at her determination. There
were not nearly enough missionaries to staff even
the existing mission stations, let alone possible new
ones.

In answer to these objections, spoken and un-
spoken, Mary sat down and wrote a formal letter
to be read at the forthcoming meeting of the
mission council in Calabar. She set down her
own plans for the future.

"For the last decade the nearer reaches of the
river on which we ply have occupied a great deal
of my thoughts, but from various causes no sort of
supervision at all adequate suggested itself. So
there has been little of definite work accomplished . . .

"By January 2, 1904, I shall have been out
five years, and so my furlough would then be due,
but as I have not the slightest intention of going to
Britain . . . I am thankful to say I do not feel any
necessity for so doing . . . I propose to ask leave

from my work at Akpap for six months, during which time I should, in a very easy way, try to keep up an informal system of itinerating between Okoyong and Arochuku. Already I have seen a church and a dwelling-house built at Itu, and a school and a couple of rooms at Amasu. I have visited several towns of Enyong in the Creek, and have found good enough accommodation, as there are semi-European houses available and open for a lodging.

"I shall find my own canoe and crew, and shall stay at any given place any length of time which the circumstances suggest, so as not to tax my own strength, and members of my own family shall help in the elementary teaching in the schools. From our home here we should thus superintend the small school at Idot, and start in a small way work at Eki, and reside mostly at Itu as the base, working the Creek where the Enyong towns are on the way to the farther base at Amasu, reside there or itinerate from there among the Aro people in an easy way, and back again by Creek and Itu, home."

The letter sounded like a modest proposal for an interesting summer excursion. But reading between the lines, it revealed not only Mary Slessor's steel-like determination, but also the hardships she would have to face. She was fifty-six years of age, and many a time near to death through exposure, fever, or lack of proper food. She was proposing

to spend day after day for half a year canoeing
under the hot sun, sleeping in any native house
that would offer her shelter for the night, and
travelling over unknown territory extending for
thousands of square miles.

She invited her friends Mr. and Mrs. Wilkie
to come up and explore the new land for themselves, along with her. They camped in the half-
finished church at Itu. Mrs. Wilkie's camp bed
was put at one end of the church, while Mary
settled down on her sofa at the other end, with the
children all round her on mats on the floor. Mr.
Wilkie found shelter for the night in a hut in the
town. The Itu people were in turmoil because of
the soldiers who were still stationed there, keeping
open the waterway to Aro. They turned to the
missionaries for protection and advice, recognising
that they were their friends.

The travellers heard tales of the slave-market
that reinforced all Mary Slessor's arguments.
Before the breaking of the Aro power, scores of
slaves had regularly been sold off at Itu beach.
Young men were especially in demand, and the
Efiks from Calabar bought them as paddlers for
their canoes on trading expeditions.

Slowly the missionaries made their way by
canoe up the winding Creek, lovely with water-
lilies and feathery, overhanging bamboos. They
visited some of the towns of Arochuku, saw that

all was going well at Amasu, and then came back down the Enyong. At one riverside village they paid a visit to an old chief. After mutual greetings and some talk he rose suddenly and went into his dark hut. When he came out he carried a small tin box which he laid at Mary's feet. He opened it and brought out a slate, an elementary school reader, and a Bible.

Mary Slessor took them up and turned over the pages. "Where did you get these, Ete?" (father) she asked. He told her that since there was no missionary near him, he had sent his little boy, his only son, down to Calabar so that he could be educated and come back and teach his own people. The boy had died two months before.

"Now there is no one to teach us," he said. "Will you not send someone to tell us about God?"

As the canoe slid softly through the water on the way down-river Mary Slessor turned to Mr. Wilkie.

"You see, now, why I *must* go?" she said.

6

THE ENYONG CREEK

THE stalwart African paddlers sang as they thrust the canoe down the winding Enyong Creek. Mary Slessor lay back in her deck-chair under a canopy of native mats and dreamed her dreams. She had been visiting Amasu where the new school was thriving in the village palaver shed. At every town on the banks of the Enyong the villagers waved from the beach as the canoe passed. She could see the women with their water pots on their heads, and the naked children splashing in the shallows. Mary shouted a greeting in reply as the canoe slid swiftly past. In her mind's eye she could see a church and school in each of the towns of the Ibibio people, along the riverside and deep in the forest. In imagination she planned the future . . . a centre at Itu, with house and church and school, and regular trips by canoe to and from Arochuku, stopping at each beach on the way.

The Creek was as quiet and lovely as a pond beneath a blue sky. Every turn and twist revealed floating beds of water lilies, their waxen cups open to the sun. Kingfishers skimmed the stream ahead of the canoe as if leading the way, and every now and then a shout from one of the paddlers drew her attention to a snake swimming swiftly across the water. It was difficult to realise that this waterway had seen so much human misery, canoe-load after canoe-load of men, women and children in chains carried down-river like cattle to the slave-mart at Itu.

Suddenly a small canoe shot out from the bank and cut across their bows. There was a bump that made Mary Slessor sit up and abruptly banished her day-dreams. A sturdy African youth was standing in the swaying smaller canoe holding out a letter.

"Greetings, Ma," he said. "My master wants to speak with you. He has sent me to bring you to his house. Here is his letter of welcome."

Mary signalled to her paddlers to follow the messenger and the canoe nosed its way into a still smaller creek almost hidden from view in the overhanging trees. In a little they came to a sandy beach where a man and woman waited to greet them with a smile and a word of welcome. They helped Mary from the canoe and led her to a neat house furnished in European style. Greatly wondering, Mary sat down and listened to the strange story her host had to tell.

His name was Onoyom Iya Nya. He was a man of the Enyong Creek, a farmer and trader. When he was a little boy he had often seen the fighting that went on between one town and another, and he shared the terror which the Long Juju of Arochuku inspired.

One day, when he was about ten years old, he told Mary Slessor, he saw a canoe coming slowly up the Enyong Creek. In it were two white men. He had never seen white people before, and he stood stock-still in fear and amazement. They beached their canoe where he stood, and asked him in the native tongue to lead them to the chief of his town. The boy obeyed, and everyone in the place gathered round to hear what the strangers had to say. They were missionaries on an exploring trip from Calabar, and when the chief heard that he was very angry. Ibibio land, like Arochuku, was closed to the foreigner, whether Efik or European. He ordered them out of his village at once, and turned on Onoyom, shouting that he would be flogged to death for bringing the strangers there. The white men saw that they could do no good that time, but they agreed to go only if Onoyom were spared.

As he grew up Onoyom went to market and learned to trade. He travelled up the Creek to the market-places of Arochuku and down to Itu. He made a lot of money and bought slaves to work for him. But when the government officers began to come inland to find out about Arochuku and what went on there, Onoyom told them nothing. Like all his people he pretended to know nothing of the Long Juju and its slave-trade.

But the day came when he could pretend ignorance no longer. Because he was now an important man in the community, he was summoned to Itu and closely questioned by a government officer. This time he told all he knew of the country and the people and the secret paths of the forest. As a result, he was appointed guide to the Aro Expedition and ordered to lead the troops to the site of the Long Juju. Only when the whole of Aro country was under control was he allowed to return home.

About this time misfortune fell heavily on Onoyom Iya Nya. True, he was wealthy, and a head man among his people. But his only child died, his home was burned down, and in a frenzy of grief he proclaimed vengeance on the evil person who had done him such harm, as he believed, by witchcraft. In the depths of his despair he met by chance a Christian from Calabar, a former mission teacher. He spoke to him of God, and urged him to go to the "white Ma" at Itu and seek help from her.

*   *   *

Such was the story that Onoyom Iya Nya

poured out to Mary Slessor. From that moment he knew that he had found a true friend, and she in turn felt sure that God had led them both to this meeting. Onoyom became a Christian and found the peace of heart he had sought so earnestly. He devoted his strength, his influence and his wealth to help his people.

Rarely had Mary met anyone who sought so earnestly to serve God. Onoyom began to hold morning and evening prayers in his own yard, just as the "white Ma" did. Then he resolved to build a church in his town, not simply a mud and wattle hut, but a building of the finest materials to the glory of God. The timber for the work, he decided, would come from some huge "juju" trees which grew on his land. His townspeople were horrified. They cried out that some terrible disaster would fall on them if the sacred trees were cut down. The spirits would send sickness and death upon their village for such impiety. They begged Onoyom not to do this dreadful thing. But he stood firm in his resolve. When they saw that, many of the people fled from the town as if it were accursed, and settled elsewhere. Onoyom could bring death upon himself if he cared.

The courageous Christian trader sent for a sawyer and carpenter, men from faraway Gold Coast who were unaffected by the local superstitions. The sacred trees were felled, sawn and planed to make the pews and pulpit of the new church. At last, when all was ready, Onoyom Iya Nya sent word to Calabar, offering his church to the mission and asking for a teacher to be sent up to open a school.

On November 26, 1905, the missionaries and many of the Christians of Calabar came up the river by launch to the opening ceremony. Onoyom's village was gay with flags, he and his household were in their best clothes, and there were visitors present from many of the other Enyong towns, curious to see what was going on. Many of the older folk gazed with wonder at Onoyom as he received his guests. He was still alive and well. The spirits had not yet taken vengeance. But still they foretold disaster.

With deep thankfulness Mary Slessor bowed her head in prayer in the newly-dedicated church that day. Here was living proof, before all the people, that her work on the Enyong Creek was led by God. The mission council gave her their blessing and encouraged her to continue as a pioneer into new territory. Government officials, who were busy planning roads to link one town with another throughout Ibibio land, sought her advice. Once again she was asked to take on the duties of a magistrate as Vice-President of the Itu Native Court. Traders, both African and European, came to her home at Itu to ask her about markets in the interior to which they could send their goods.

Meanwhile Miss Slessor lived as simply as she had always done, in a native house in Itu. Visitors of an evening would find her in her rocking-chair, nursing a wakeful child in her arms. All round the room were soap-box cradles for twin or orphan babies, the children wrapped up in brown paper for blankets or in old newspapers. Mary herself laid down a cement floor in the hut while Janie whitewashed the walls. The cement was to keep out the ants, which in Africa can speedily make a house uninhabitable. Someone once asked Mary what she knew about making cement.

"I don't know how to make it," she replied. "I just stir it like porridge, turn it out, smooth it with a stick, and all the time keep praying: 'Lord, here's the cement; if to Thy glory, set it,' and it has never once gone wrong!"

All day long, and far into the night, there was an endless stream of visitors. Some came to lay a case before her for judgment, a family quarrel or a dispute about land. Others gathered for a reading lesson, or to ask her to explain something from the Bible to them. Many sought healing for their sores. They came from far and near, from Aro-chuku, from the villages of Ibibio, and even from her old home in Okoyong. And for everyone she had a word of welcome and advice and a prayer for their well-being.

Good news came from Calabar. A member of an Edinburgh church had offered to provide a hospital, dispensary and all the necessary equipment as a tribute to Mary Slessor's work. The mission council decided that the hospital should be at Itu and a doctor was to be sent up as soon as possible to be in charge. Once again Mary felt that she must move on. Always she led the way and others came to build up the work she had begun.

*   *   *

Already there was a chain of little churches and schools stretching into the interior, reaching out to the teeming towns of Arochuku. There came continual requests for teachers and evangelists. In a letter home to Scotland Mary wrote of what had been accomplished in so short a time: "First Itu, then the Creek, then back from Aro, where I had set my heart, to a solitary wilderness of the most forbidding description, where the silence of the bush has never been broken, and here before three months are past there are miles of roads, and miles and miles more all surveyed and being worked upon by gangs of men from everywhere, and free labour is being created and accepted as quickly as even a novelist could imagine."

71

But there was news of Arochuku. One of the other missionaries had toured not only the riverside villages of Enyong but also the towns of Aro, following in Mary Slessor's footsteps. Eagerly she read his report to the mission council:

"Close to Arochuku, within a circle the diameter of which is less than three miles, there are nineteen large towns. I have visited sixteen of these, each of which is as large as or larger than Creek Town. The people are a stalwart race, far in advance of Efik. The majority are very anxious for help. A section is strongly opposed, even to the point of persecuting those who under the influence of Miss Slessor and others have already begun to try to live 'in God's fashion'. This opposition seems to be one of the most helpful signs, as proving that there will at least be no indifference. The head chief of all the Aros, who was the chief formerly in control of the Long Juju at Arochuku, is one of those most favourable. He has already announced to the other chiefs his intention to rule in God's ways. He has been the most keen in asking the missionary to come. A new church will be built, and he offers to build a house for any missionary who comes."

Mary's heart was torn between Ibibio and Arochuku. What a huge country it was, and she one frail woman! Two things helped her to make up her mind. The first was that a missionary was sent to live in Arochuku with the promise that other missionaries would join him later. The other deciding factor was the opening up of Ibibio land. A network of roads was rapidly covering the hitherto dense forest. To Mary they were highways for the Gospel of Jesus Christ.

Now that Itu was to be a properly staffed Mission station and hospital, Miss Slessor moved her household from Itu to Ikot-Obong, about five miles inland. Once more she had to build a home, start a school and church, set up a dispensary. But for the first time in Africa she lived beside a road. No longer did she need to trek day in day out on foot through the forest. A bicycle was the answer to her need now. It came as a present from the District Commissioner. What excitement there was in Ikot-Obong when Ma Slessor mounted it for the first time and wobbled up and down the dusty road! "Enañ ukwak," they called it . . . the "iron cow". Mary was thrilled. "Fancy an old woman like me on a cycle!" she wrote. "The new road makes it easy to ride, and I'm running up and down and taking a new bit in a village two miles off. It has done me all the good in the world, and I will soon be able to overtake more work."

A still greater thrill was to come. A government official roared up to her door one day in a motor-car, to the wonder and delight of the missionary and her household. Many a time the car was put at her disposal, with an African driver, and she was able to visit outlying schools and churches quickly and without utterly exhausting herself.

*   *   *

Meanwhile her friend Onoyom Iya Nya had never faltered in his faith. The school and church in his town prospered and the doleful prophecies of the older folk were still unfulfilled. Then, with the wet season, the Enyong river began to rise. The rains were exceptionally severe that year, and they wrought havoc far across the country. Day after day the flood waters rose, until they overflowed the banks and spread like a lake over the fields of growing yams. The people waited in fear. Surely this was the long-delayed punishment of Onoyom's rash act in cutting down the sacred trees? The waters crept through the village and flowed into the houses, so that the people had to take refuge in their canoes. Soon the whole place was under water, with only the roofs of the houses and the new church in sight. With a sore heart Onoyom one day floated right through the open door of the church in a small canoe and saw the muddy flood covering the splendid pews and reaching to the pulpit.

Now even some of his friends turned against

74

him, while his enemies were triumphant. "You see what a disaster you have brought on us!" they cried. "Our crops are ruined, our homes gone. We told you to leave this new teaching alone, but you wouldn't listen. Will you listen now, and go back to the customs of our fathers and make peace with the spirits?"

In his sorrow and loneliness of spirit Onoyom sought out Ma Slessor once again. Was it true what the people said? he asked her. Or was God punishing him?

"I think it is the hand of God leading you to better things," said Mary. "Why don't you build a new town, a clean town, tidy and beautiful? Perhaps that is what God is trying to show you."

Onoyom caught at the idea with delight. At the very height of the floods he marked out the parts of his land which were still high and dry. Then, as the waters went down, he announced his plan. They would rebuild their town, houses and school and church on the high ground. It meant months of heavy toil, clearing the forest, levelling the land, laying out the streets. But before the rains came again the new town was finished. It was clean, well-spaced and tidy, and in the centre was Onoyom's own house, the church and the school, with a spacious playground for the children.

With a flash of inspiration Onoyom gave the place a new name—Obio Usiere, the Town of the Dawn. It was a city set on a hill, a place where God was honoured.

7

ON TO IKPE

"I DARE not go back!" That was Mary Slessor's cry as she set herself to the conquest of a vast stretch of new country for Christ. But her furlough was long overdue, and so weak was she with fatigue and frequent illness that she could scarcely drag herself about. For a time she thought that perhaps the children could push her about in an invalid chair, but by and by the government doctor made it quite plain to her that she would die if she did not go home.

So in the middle of May, 1907, she sailed from Duke Town. This time she took with her a little African boy, Dan McArthur Slessor, who was about eight years old. Janie was left in charge of the other children. Miss Slessor was amazed to find herself famous all over Scotland. All she wanted to do was to rest quietly in the home of a friend, but soon letters and invitations began to come in from every part of the country, asking her to come and speak about her work.

This frail little old woman, who had fearlessly faced all the dangers of the African bush, was so shy that she could scarcely bring herself to address a meeting of her own folk. "I am trembling for the meetings," she wrote, "but surely God will help me. It is His own cause." She hated to hear her work praised as if hers were the glory of it. It was God's work, and she was only His weak, humble servant. Once at a meeting of ministers she gave an impressive address which was followed by a hearty vote of thanks. Fiercely she turned to the minister who had praised her and cried: "Instead of thanking me, I wish any of you had said: 'Let us pray for the work in Calabar.'"

One of her visits was to Dundee, where she had been brought up. There, to her delight, she met some of her old friends who had worked with her in the Sunday School when she was a girl, thirty-five years before. They walked along the old familiar roads and talked of all that God had done for them. It was the last time Mary Slessor was ever to see her native land.

In November, 1907, after only a few months' furlough, she was back again in Africa. The mission had taken over her house at Ikot-Obong, with two lady missionaries in charge. It was to become a training centre for girls, as Mary Slessor had planned. She herself moved on with her household to yet another site. She chose a plot of ground at Use, on high land above the road between Ikot-Obong and Itu. Once again she was builder, carpenter, and cement-mixer. A friend who came to stay with her found Mary Slessor living in a single room, her bed a mattress placed on a sheet of corrugated iron on the floor. The visitor was anxious to be up early one morning, but there was no alarm clock. That was no trouble to Mary. She tied a young cockerel to the foot of her guest's camp-bed and said: "There's your alarm clock! He'll waken you all right!"

Use was a lonely spot, the haunt of leopards. Often Mary came home late at night from her visits to outlying villages. Sometimes a leopard stood in her path, its eyes glittering. Dan, who was usually with her, was terrified. But Ma Slessor tore a stick from the bush and marched forward fearlessly, shoo-ing the wild beast away.

One day they were travelling on the Enyong Creek, Mary stretched out on the floor of the canoe with the children sitting cross-legged beside her. She was quietly reading when there was a sudden shout of alarm from the paddlers. "Ma! Se Isantim!" ("Ma! Look, a hippo!") Her first thought was of the children, lest in sudden fright one of them should jump up and upset the frail canoe. Carefully she rose to her full height and lifted a bamboo pole. She threw it like a spear at the hippo's ugly head, shouting "Go away, you!" To the amazement of the paddlers the huge beast dived and disappeared. They talked about it for many days afterwards, and the story spread far and wide in the villages of the Creek. The boy Dan never forgot these incidents or what Ma Slessor said to him: "Dan, my son, never allow weakness or fear to overpower you. I know these places are full of danger, but if I were to admit weakness, I might as well pack up and go home to Scotland."

*   *   *

Mary Slessor now fought a constant battle against pain and weariness. Though the government motor-car was available to take her from place to place along the main roads, there were many villages in the forest which could only be reached on foot or by bicycle. Everywhere she went she had to take Dan or one of the other lads with her to push her bicycle up the hills and to help her across the rushing streams. Continually she lay wakeful at night, racked with pain. Only heavy doses of laudanum kept her from going off her head. An occasional visit to the hospital at Itu, or to Duke Town, allowed her to rest, but as soon as she felt a little better Mary went back to Use.

One thing that delighted her at Duke Town was the growth of the training institution. Some sixteen years before she had written a stirring letter to the Church in Scotland pleading for the setting up of a training centre for boys and young men. Both government and mission had backed up her pleas and the result was a spacious institution on the hill at Duke Town. Boys from the towns and villages throughout Okoyong, Ibibio, Arochuku, Itu and far beyond eagerly sought admission. They went back to their own communities as trained teachers, clerks, carpenters, engineers, blacksmiths or tailors. Mary Slessor's heart rejoiced in the change from the old days of drinking, fighting and slave-dealing. Some day, she hoped, just as much might be done for girls in Ikot-Obong or Use. She herself might not live to see it, but as a pioneer she could make plans and point the way.

Meanwhile, her work in the bush went on, as her unconquerable spirit forced her tired, pain-racked body to the duties of each day. The house still overflowed with outcast twins and orphaned children. Still she held regular classes to train lads and girls as teachers and evangelists. The Court took up hours of her time.

*   *   *

One morning a young man appeared at Use, naked, except for a strip of loin-cloth. Behind him was a group of men, all strangers to Mary Slessor.

"Greetings, Ma!" said the youth. "We have come from our town to ask you to visit us and start a school."

"Where do you come from?" asked Mary with quick interest.

The lad waved a hand in the direction of the Creek. "Two days' journey by canoe and through the bush," he said. "Our town is called Ikpe. There are very many people there, and a big market."

"A big market?" repeated Mary. "Why have the Calabar traders never told me about it?"

"We don't allow the Efik men to come into our land," was the reply. "It is a closed market. We don't want strangers. But the white men marched from Arochuku with their guns and made us afraid. That is why some of us have come to you for help. Come with us now and we will build a house for you to teach book."

Mary sighed. Her fame and authority had reached out far and wide, but the people could not or would not realise that she was an old woman, unable to get about as once she had done. But the call to adventure in Christ's name was there, and her heart responded though her body rebelled.

"I'll come," she promised. "No, not now, but I'll come soon."

The journey to Ikpe was a long and tedious one.

First there was a day by canoe up the winding Enyong Creek, far past the beaches for Arochuku. Next day a weary tramp through the forest brought her to the town of the big market. Ikpe was a bustling place, indeed, as the messenger had said. To her surprise the young men had already begun to put up a mud church with a rest-room for herself, confident that she would come as she had promised. Curious crowds of naked children swarmed about her. Only the old chiefs were indifferent to her arrival, fearing interference with their customs.

For several days she stayed there, living on the food the people brought her. Ikpe was one of the most heathen places she had ever seen, the people naked and uncouth, the dark huts swarming with flies and mosquitoes. But to Mary it was a new centre of opportunity, and already in her mind's eye she saw a mission station there. She explored the district on foot, noting the many villages within walking distance of the market. She wondered how she could work Use and Ikpe together.

"If only there were two of me!" she thought. "Then one could live here and go up and down to Arochuku. The other could carry on at Use and make a home for the twin-mothers and the girls."

But alas! there was only one Mary Slessor, and

a very frail one at that. When she got back to Use she was ill for weeks with the exertion of the journey. The young men of Ikpe would not let her be. They sent deputation after deputation down the Creek to ask: "When are you coming to live with us?" They told her that services were being held regularly in their little church, but there was no one to teach them God's way.

Several times she made the trip, paying a fleeting visit, longing for the mission to establish a permanent centre at Ikpe. Letters began to come down to Duke Town, passed from messenger to messenger, pleading for support for her venture in this hitherto unheard-of place.

"One can't do much amid schoolboys and visitors and sick folk and a household," she wrote. "Long, sleepless nights are now my portion. As the shadows lengthen and so much lies to be sorted out before the sun goes down, one's energies are watched over like a miser's hoard. I tell you that I am pledged to two towns close on ten miles of hill track away and that this district is absolutely beyond me; and that villages all round are crying out for help . . . not to speak of a congregation unshepherded at Use . . ."

Then, with a characteristic flash of humour she apologises for her uneven writing: "My apology for the apparent slovenliness of this, but I've had a fractious, newly-vaccinated baby on my knee under the pad, and she does not like it more than I do!"

*   *   *

She made up her mind to remove her whole household to Ikpe for the time being, though still keeping in touch with Use. A canoe brought up materials for a house, corrugated iron sheets for the walls and roof, timber for doors and windows. Scores of men turned out to clear a site and level the ground for the new building, and Mary darted here, there and everywhere to supervise the work. It was like beginning her missionary life all over again. But she was no longer young and full of vigour. She was sixty-three years of age, feeble, and alone. "It is borne in on one here," she wrote, "that 'not by might, nor by power, but by My Spirit,' is the only leverage. Man, and Mary Slessor, are simply nothing."

The mission council was opposed to Ikpe as a new station. For one thing, they simply had not enough missionaries to follow up the work that Mary Slessor had begun. For another, they realised that she would kill herself if she went on as she was doing. Their strongest argument, however, was that Ikpe was too unhealthy a spot for any white man or woman to stay there permanently.

In January 1912 a young missionary doctor who had been barely a year in the country was sent up to Ikpe to see for himself what conditions were like and to bring back a medical report. His name was Dr. John W. Hitchcock, and he was to become a notable missionary in Calabar. He at once fell under the spell of Mary Slessor's personality, and she in turn loved him like a son. But he was adamant about Ikpe. The site of the mission house was unsuitable. The rains of the wet season had made the place a filthy swamp. Dirt, damp and mosquitoes made it an impossible place to live in.

Mary Slessor was disposed to argue, and to stay on at Ikpe in defiance of everyone. But her over-wrought body gave way, and she was forced to return to Use, where Dr. Hitchcock walked up from the hospital at Itu every other day to visit her. He absolutely forbade her to travel anywhere for the time being, and for once, because of her admiration for the young man and his work, Mary was constrained to listen to reason.

"A rare man," she said. "A rare Christian, a rare doctor. A physician for soul and body."

He, in turn, with all his admiration for her, found it very hard to get her to obey his instructions. Her heart was weak, and rest was essential. He suspected, too, that she was not getting enough nourishing food.

"You must eat meat twice a day," he insisted.

"I never eat much meat, Doctor," was Mary's reply.

In answer to that he sent up a fowl from Itu, with his compliments. Next day she protested. "Why did you send that fowl, Doctor?"

His only answer was: "Because it could not come itself!"

Her one desire was to get back to Ikpe. Dr. Hitchcock said it was unthinkable for many weeks. She must never cycle again, he told her, or trek long distances through the bush. In answer to that she got the gift of a basket-chair on wheels, in which the boys could push her about. In it she trundled up and down the roads from Use, stopping at each village to visit the school or to discuss plans for further extension. But it could not last. She became too weak even to leave her couch. She had been thirty-six years a missionary, and now she was growing deaf, short-sighted, crippled with rheumatism, and very, very tired.

"I'm lame, and feeble and foolish," she wrote of herself. "The wrinkles are wonderful, no concertina is so wonderfully folded and convoluted, I'm a wee, wee wifie, verra little buikit . . . but I grip on well, none the less." And grip on she did, for there was still work to be done.

8

THE LIFE THAT MADE MELODY

AFTER a long, hot day in the wards of Itu hospital, Dr. Hitchcock would tramp up the winding, dusty road through the forest to Use to keep an eye on Mary Slessor. There was tea on the veranda, with a big box for a table and milk-boxes for seats. Mary was always delighted to see him. While Janie spread a clean towel over the "table" by way of a cloth, the two missionaries talked of the latest news from Duke Town or from faraway Britain. The meal usually consisted of water biscuits spread with strawberry jam, and cup after cup of tea. There was only one knife between them. All round them on the veranda the children played and quarrelled and were scolded or comforted by "Ma".

"You must get away from here and have a real rest," insisted the doctor.

"I'm not going home, if that's what you mean," said Mary firmly. "I haven't the time, and there's so much to do."

"Well, then," suggested Dr. Hitchcock, "come down and stay with me at Itu for a week or two.

I'll feed you up with palm-oil chop. Then you can go down to Duke Town and let Dr. Adams of the Government Hospital have a look at you. He'll soon tell you what you're fit for."

Dr. Adams knew Miss Slessor of old, and he was just as emphatic as Dr. Hitchcock. "You must get out of the tropics for a bit, into a healthier climate," he urged. "Take the next boat to the Canary Islands. Spend a month there in peace and quiet, and you'll be a new woman when you come back."

Mary hesitated. She hated to leave the folk who needed her so much at Use and Ikpe. But perhaps if she took a short holiday now she would not need a furlough next year. She made up her mind to go. Janie would go with her to look after her.

So began the most wonderful holiday Mary Slessor ever had in her busy life. The captain and officers of the ship treated her as the most famous person they had ever had as a passenger, as indeed she was. Government officials at every port of call along the Coast came on board to pay their respects, bringing flowers and baskets of fresh fruit as tribute of their affection. Many of them had known her in Calabar years before when they were "young laddies", as she called them, at the beginning of their service.

They were a strange pair of visitors at the

luxury hotel in Grand Canary, the frail little old lady with the broad Scots accent, and the timid black girl who always attended her. When they landed on the island Mary Slessor was still too weak to walk up the slightest slope. But a fort-night later the quiet beauty of the place and the fresh, invigorating air had worked a miraculous change. Every morning she climbed to the top of the hill behind the hotel and sat there in the sunshine with the strong sea-breeze blowing in her face. Lunch and tea were sent up to her, and she spent all day there in utter peace of body and spirit.

*   *   *

When she got back to Calabar Dr. Adams highly approved of the change in his old friend. "You're good for many years yet," he said, "but you must take care of yourself." Mary Slessor made her way up to Use with lots of good advice ringing in her ears, but soon she was working twice as hard to make up for the time she had been away. Once again she made regular trips to Ikpe, some-times by canoe, and sometimes in the government motor-car by a circuitous route that took her within five miles of her house there. A letter from Ikpe in January 1913 shows her back at the old familiar round:

"I have a few minutes to spare this morning between the turns of water they are carrying for the washing. Our vessels are few and they run to the spring between times. I can write only a few lines, then I'm off to the tub. It is Saturday, and no school, so we always wash here on that day, as water carrying is heavy . . ."

Later, in the same letter: "A number of visitors on Saturday kept me from getting more done. We had a good Sunday, and all the girls who had been bothered by the chiefs to make play and sacrifice were in their places at Church, which was a great comfort and joy to me. Yesterday passed with school and sick folk, and to-day, Tuesday, is market-day, with lots of Enyong visitors, and a good big school. I shall send this letter with the policeman who watches the market, so that the clerk at the nearest court can send it on for postage to the District Court, twenty-five miles on."

Apart from her African household, she was completely on her own, as remote from her fellow-missionaries as if she had been in another world.

"I have been here seven weeks," she wrote once, "without one scrap of paper from the outside—letter or paper—nothing to read but the old advertisement sheets of papers lining the press and the boxes." The Bible was her constant solace. She got up as soon as it was light, about half-past five, and studied her Bible sentence by sentence, seeking its deepest meaning, and writing her thoughts in the margin. Her Bible notes and the outlines of sermons she wrote are still preserved in Dundee to-day.

But Mary Slessor was not forgotten in Calabar Her friends in government and mission alike talked and wrote of her magnificent pioneer work. And in July 1913 Mary Slessor was summoned to Duke Town to receive the silver cross of the Order of the Hospital of St. John of Jerusalem, of which she had been elected an Honorary Associate.

It was an ordeal for her to come down from lonely Ikpe and face the crowds which gathered for the formal presentation. A government launch was sent for her, and at the Barracks in Duke Town there was a reception in her honour. The whole of the European community of Calabar was present. She was fêted like a queen. But when the Provincial Commissioner placed the ribbon of the Order round her neck, and everyone hushed to hear her reply, Mary Slessor said simply: "If I have done anything in my life it has been easy, because the Master has gone before."

*　　　*　　　*

Mary herself was glad to escape to Ikpe, away

from the praise and publicity. There was so much still to be done. The thought of thousands of folk all round her who had never heard the gospel weighed heavily on her mind. "The last time I was in the school," she wrote, "I counted eight hundred women and girls running past in eager competition to secure the best places at the fishing-grounds where the men had been working all the morning, and these are but a fraction of our womankind. But what can I do with supervision of the school and church and dispensary and household?" What she did was to go on trek again, in defiance of doctor's orders, travelling far and wide in her "box on wheels" to visit more and more villages which had never seen a missionary. She was a pioneer to the last.

Mary Slessor was back in Use for Christmas, 1914, her African family about her. She was very weak, very tired. Early in January fever seized her again, and the girls sent for her missionary friends from Ikot-Obong and for the Itu doctor. The whole household gathered to watch over their beloved Ma in the simple mud house with the cement floor, iron roof, and few sticks of furniture. In the hour before the dawn on January 13, 1915, her life slipped quietly away.

The sound of wailing and lament was heard far and wide in the forest as the news spread. The mission launch *Diamond* came up from Calabar to bring her body down to Duke Town for burial and the whole town was present at the simple funeral service. In the fresh-dug earth of the grave was planted a cutting from a rose-bush at Use, a fragrant reminder of a life wholly dedicated to God.

To-day, a huge cross of rugged Scottish granite marks the last resting-place of Mary Mitchell Slessor on the hillside above Duke Town. By the side of the road at Use a simple cairn reminds the passer-by of her home there. In the church of her up-bringing in Dundee magnificent stained-glass windows portray scenes from her daily life in Africa.

*   *   *

But her true memorial lies not in radiant glass or grey granite. The influence of Mary Slessor lives on in the towns and villages of Calabar to-day. It lives in the Slessor Memorial Home in Arochuku, where girls are trained to make happy, healthful homes. It lives in the Hope Waddell Training Institution which she did much to inspire, and which sends out young men far and wide throughout Nigeria to serve their fellow-man as teachers, ministers, doctors, lawyers, agriculturalists and government officials. It lives in the care of twins and twin-mothers, of sick folk and lepers which still goes on throughout the Calabar Mission. The tradition of her life of service goes on in the churches, hospitals and schools which grew up behind her pioneering footsteps.

In a letter written to young people in Scotland not long before she died, Mary Slessor appealed to others to follow where she had led: "Gird yourself for the battle outside somewhere, and keep your heart young. Give up your whole being to create music everywhere, in the light places and in the dark places, and your life will make melody. I'm a witness to the perfect joy and satisfaction of a single life . . . with a tail of human tag-rag hanging on. It is rare! Mine has been such a joyous service. God has been good to me, letting me serve Him in this humble way. I cannot thank Him enough for the honour He conferred upon me when He sent me to the Dark Continent."

In that faith in her Lord she lived and worked, always . . . mill-girl, missionary, housewife, explorer, magistrate, pioneer, heroine, saint. Perhaps the best description of her in a few words is a verse from the Psalms, which says: "Thou hast given me the shield of thy salvation: Thy right hand hath holden me up, and Thy gentleness hath made me great."